Mills and big wheels

Peter Firmin

A & C Black · London

Contents

About this book 3

Glossary 4

Tools, equipment and materials 5

Useful tips 6

Wind power 8
    A weathervane 8
    Stick windmills 9
    The simple windmill 10

Wind and pulley power 12
    The fixed windmill 14
    The wind-powered roundabout 16

Water power 18
    The "overshot" waterwheel 18

Water and pulley power 20
    The water-powered Ferris wheel 22

Sand power 24
    The sand wheel 26
    The sand-powered sawmill 28

People 30

Roundabout rides 31

Decorating your models 32

With grateful thanks to the following people who helped to make the models for this book: Dorian, Lewis, Ruth, Olivia, Sam, Laurence and Oliver.

A CIP catalogue record for this book is available from the British Library.

First published 1994 by A & C Black (Publishers) Limited
35 Bedford Row, London WC1R 4JH

ISBN 0-7136-3623-8

Filmset by Rowland Phototypesetting Limited
Bury St Edmunds, Suffolk
Printed in Great Britain by
Cambus Litho Limited, East Kilbride

About this book

In this book, there are detailed instructions to help you make windmills, waterwheels, sand wheels and many other working models. Some of the models make use of pulleys. You can create a more complicated model such as the wind-powered roundabout or the water-powered Ferris wheel by using a band of thick wool to link the pulleys on two models. Before you begin, take time to read the instructions for the models carefully. Look at the illustrations, too, before you set to work. Some of the models will take time to make, so don't try to do everything in one go.

On page 5 there's a list of things you will need. It's a good idea to have two large boxes to put everything in – one for all your materials and one for your tools. Most of the materials you will need are things you can find around the house; things which would normally be thrown away. Large boxes and cardboard tubes are often thrown away by shops. The larger your selection of boxes, the more varied and interesting your models will be, so start collecting.

You will need to buy some materials, such as PVA glue and wire. But you can save money by sharing these and your tools with friends.

I hope you'll have fun making and using these models. Why not try inventing and making some models of your own?

Glossary

This glossary explains some of the words used in the book and describes the various parts used in making the models. All words in the glossary appear in the text in **bold** type.

Axle   a wire or rod between two holes to support a **pulley** or wheel.

Bearing   a hole or tube in which an **axle** turns.

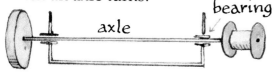

Diagonal line   a line drawn between opposite corners of a four-sided shape.

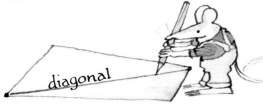

Energy   the power of doing work.

Friction   the resistance caused by two surfaces rubbing together.

Gravity   the pull of an object towards the Earth.

Horizontal movement   moving on a level plane (a turntable).

Pulley   a wheel with a groove in the rim for a rope to run over, used for turning and lifting.

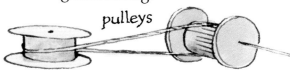

Radius   a straight line running from the centre to the edge of a circle.

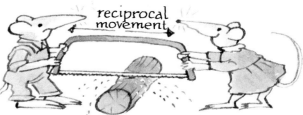

Reciprocal movement   moving backwards and forwards.

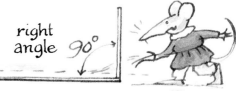

Right angle   a square corner.

Rotary movement moving round and round.

Vertical movement   moving on an upright plane (a bicycle wheel).

Washer   a bead placed between two moving parts which reduces **friction**.

4

Tools, equipment . . .

awl for making holes
block of wood
brushes
bulldog clips and pegs
coloured paints
craft knife
drawing pins
felt tips
hacksaw

hammer
knitting needle
metal ruler
needle and thread
newspaper to work on
pair of compasses
paper fasteners
pins
pliers

PVA glue
school glue
scissors
sponge for putting on paint
stapler
sticky tape
tacks
vice
white emulsion paint
wood glue

and materials

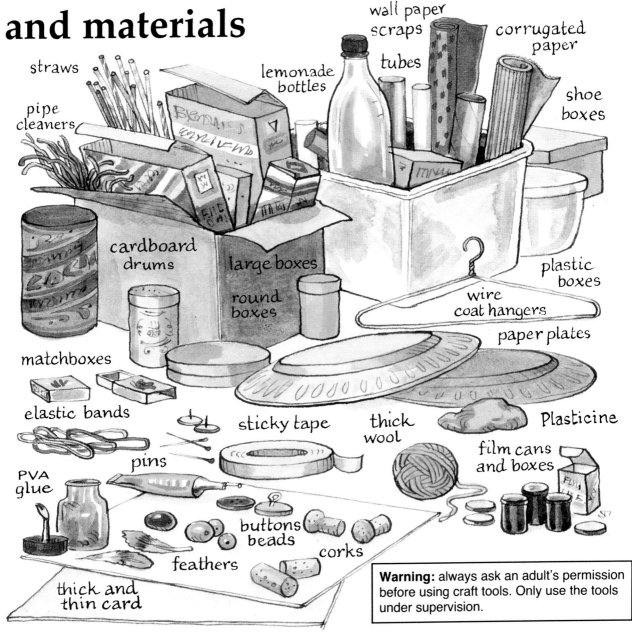

straws
pipe cleaners
wall paper scraps
tubes
corrugated paper
lemonade bottles
shoe boxes
cardboard drums
large boxes
round boxes
wire coat hangers
plastic boxes
paper plates
matchboxes
elastic bands
sticky tape
thick wool
Plasticine
film cans and boxes
PVA glue
pins
buttons beads
corks
feathers
thick and thin card

Warning: always ask an adult's permission before using craft tools. Only use the tools under supervision.

5

Useful tips

Before you begin, read these pages carefully. They will tell you which tools to use for which jobs, and how to use them safely.

Cutting

Where possible, use scissors to cut card and boxes. The best sort of scissors have rounded ends. Never point scissors at anyone.

If you want to use a craft knife, ask an adult. Make sure the knife is sharp. Protect your work surface by cutting on to a thick pad of newspaper on top of a piece of card.

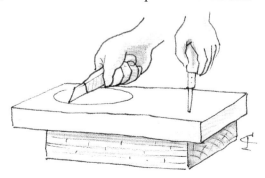

Pricking

If you are using an awl to prick holes in a box, or cutting a box with a knife, put a block of wood inside the box so you've got a hard surface to press down on.

Gluing

Use small pegs or paperclips to hold glued pieces of card together. Then you can get on with something else while the glue is drying.

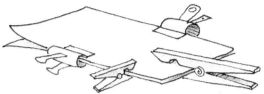

To join boxes, glue the surfaces together and tape the joins with masking tape. The models can be made stronger and are easier to paint if you paste paper over all the surfaces first.

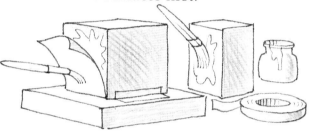

To join pieces of card, glue the surfaces together and staple the edges.

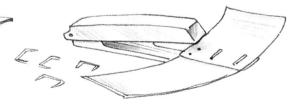

Joining pieces of plastic

To join pieces of plastic, make holes in the plastic with an awl and thread a paper fastener through the holes.

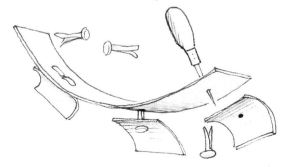

Cutting wire

Cut thin wire with pliers.

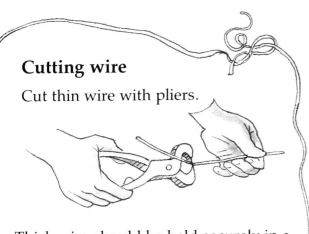

Thick wire should be held securely in a vice and cut with a hacksaw. Keep your fingers clear of the saw.

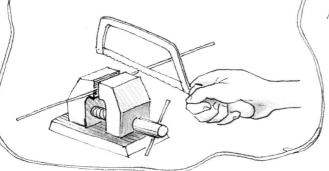

Bending card

If you want to bend a piece of card, it's best to score the card first. Place the edge of a metal ruler along the line where you want to bend the card. Pressing down firmly, run the blunt point of a knitting needle down the card, following the edge of the ruler.

Bend the card along the score line.

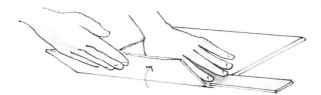

Dividing a plate into twelve

Use a pair of compasses to draw a circle a little larger than your paper plate on a sheet of paper. Make a mark anywhere on the circle and label it A. Keeping the compasses at the same **radius**, place the compass point at A and mark B.

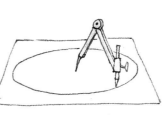
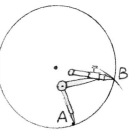

Place the compasses at B and mark C. Continue in this way until you arrive back at A. You should have six points on the circle.

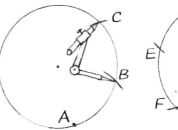
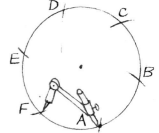

Make a mark on the circle halfway between A and B. Starting at this point make six more marks on the circle. Lay the paper plate on top of the circle and mark the twelve points on the circle on the plate.

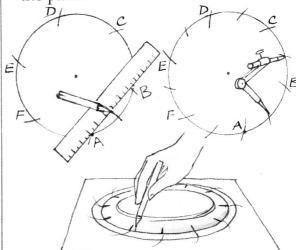

Wind power

The wind is moving air. A strong wind can lift tiles off roofs or even uproot trees. But we can use the power of the wind too.

A weathervane

A weathervane can show us the direction of the wind.

> You will need: a straw, a strip of paper about 7 × 3cm, 10cm of straight thin wire, a straight piece of coathanger wire about 7cm long, a block of wood about 10 × 10 × 2cm, a bead and some Plasticine.

1 Cut a triangle out of one end of the strip of paper.

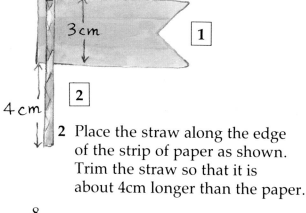

2 Place the straw along the edge of the strip of paper as shown. Trim the straw so that it is about 4cm longer than the paper.

3 Glue the edge of the strip of paper round the piece of straw.

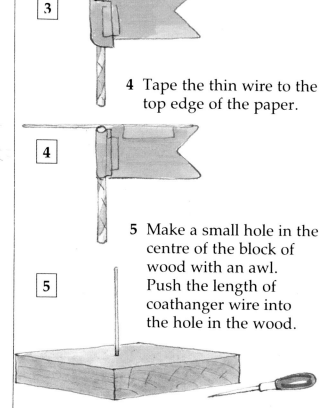

4 Tape the thin wire to the top edge of the paper.

5 Make a small hole in the centre of the block of wood with an awl. Push the length of coathanger wire into the hole in the wood.

6 Thread the bead on to the coathanger wire. The bead acts as a **washer**. Slide the straw on to the wire above the bead. To balance your weathervane, attach a small arrow of Plasticine to the free end of the wire.

Stick windmills

These two stick windmills are quick and easy to make.

Model A

You will need: 30cm of dowel, a paper plate and a pin.

1 Divide the paper plate into twelve equal sections (see page 7).

2 Cut 3cm along each dividing line.

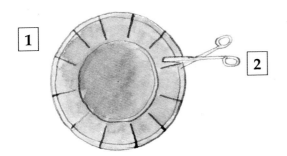

3 Bend upwards the right-hand corner of each of the twelve sections.

4 Stick a pin through the centre of the plate and into one end of the dowel.

Use a bead to make it turn more smoothly.

Model B

You will need: 30cm of dowel, a square piece of paper 20 × 20cm and a pin.

1 Draw in the **diagonal lines** on the square as shown. Mark the centre of the square.

2 Cut in 10cm from each corner.

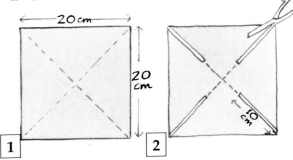

3 Fold the right-hand corner of each triangle towards the centre of the square.

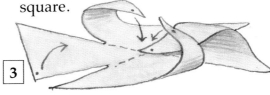

4 Pin these corners to the centre and to one end of the dowel.

The simple windmill

Windmills were invented thousands of years ago. The wind turns the sails of a windmill. The movement of the sails drives machinery inside the windmill. Today windmills are used to grind corn, pump water and drain flooded land.

> You will need: a cork, 2 straight pieces of coathanger wire, one about 20cm long the other about 30cm long, 8 cocktail sticks, 9 straws, 4 sheets of toilet tissue, a round tin eg. a cocoa drum, 2 beads, Plasticine, 6 toilet roll tubes, a cardboard box about 15 × 15 × 5cm, a strip of card about 12 × 3cm and a weathervane (see page 8).

1 Make four equally spaced holes round the top edge of the cork with an awl. Glue a cocktail stick into each hole.

2 Make four holes round the bottom of the cork in-between the holes you have already made round the top of the cork. Glue a cocktail stick into each hole.

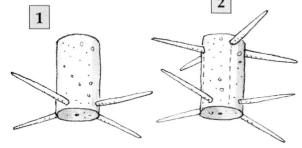

3 Slide a straw over each cocktail stick. Glue them into position.

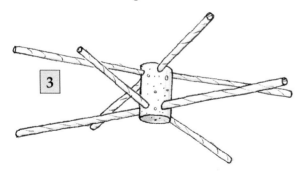

4 Glue the edge of a piece of toilet tissue to each of the straws at the top of the cork.

5 Glue the other ends of the toilet tissue to a straw at the bottom of the cork as shown.

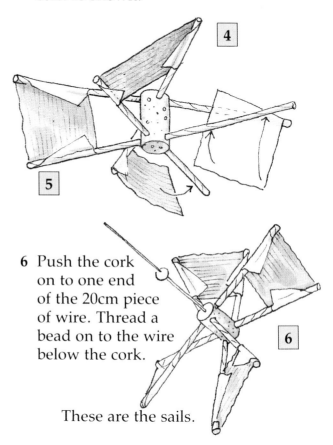

6 Push the cork on to one end of the 20cm piece of wire. Thread a bead on to the wire below the cork.

These are the sails.

7 Make a small hole with an awl in the centre of the top and the base of the round drum. Slide the drum on to the 30cm piece of wire.

8 Wrap a small piece of Plasticine round the wire at each end of the drum to stop it sliding about.

9 Make a hole in each side of the drum at A.

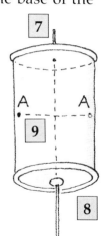

10 Tape the six toilet roll tubes together in pairs, to make three pillars. Tape the three pillars together to make one thick pillar.

10

11 Glue and tape the pillar to the centre of the cardboard box.

11

12 Push the end of the sails wire through the holes in the drum at A.

12

A

13

13 Thread a bead and a straw on to the wire below the drum.

14 Spread a little glue over the straw beneath the round drum. Push the straw down through the centre of the pillar, until the base of the drum rests on the top edge of the tower.

15 Make a weathervane for the top of the windmill (see page 8). Slide a bead on to the wire above the drum, to act as a **washer**. Slide the weathervane on to the wire above the bead.

15

The weathervane helps you to turn the sails to face into the wind.

14

Glue on a strip of card as a handle.

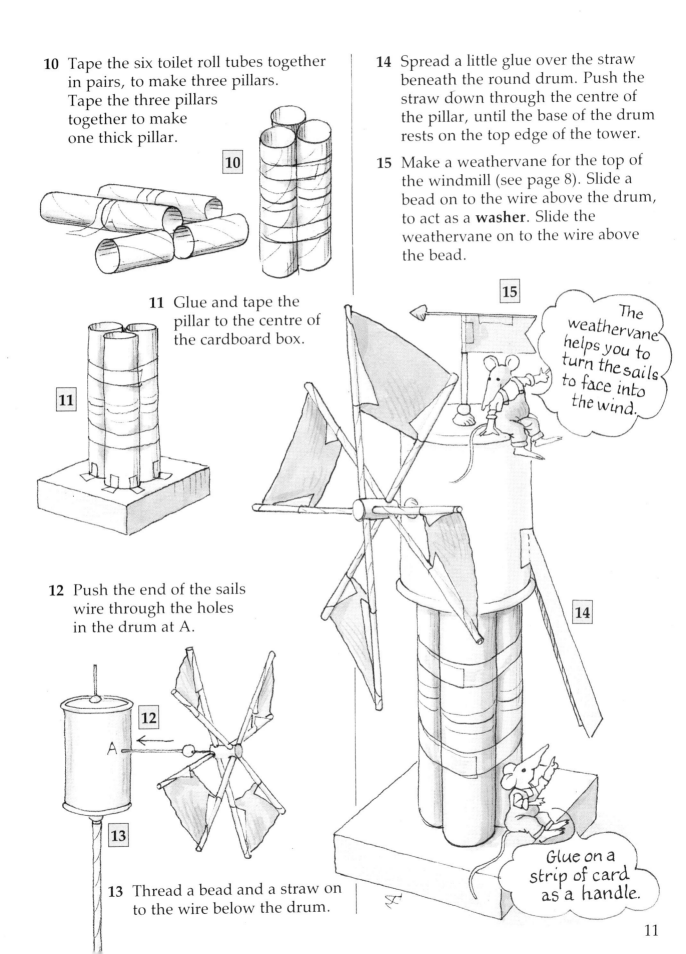

11

Wind and pulley power

By linking the small **pulley** on the fixed windmill shown here, to the large **pulley** on the roundabout, the fixed windmill will drive the roundabout. The band of thick wool which joins the two **pulleys** turns **vertical** movement into **horizontal** movement.

The band has to travel further round the large **pulley** on the roundabout than it does round the small **pulley** on the windmill. This means that the roundabout turns more slowly than the windmill.

Making the small pulley

You will need: a cork, an elastic band and a sheet of card.

1 Wrap the elastic band tightly round the cork.

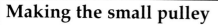

2 Draw and cut out two identical card circles. The circles should be a little larger than the cork. Glue one card circle to each end of the cork.

3 Use an awl to make a hole through the centre of the pulley

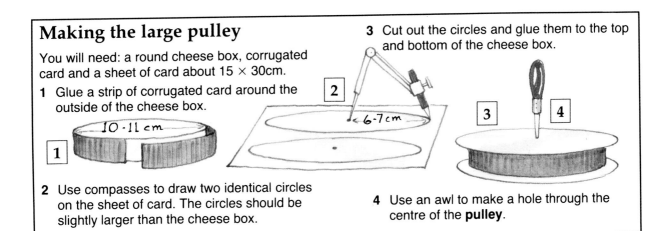

Making the large pulley

You will need: a round cheese box, corrugated card and a sheet of card about 15 × 30cm.

1 Glue a strip of corrugated card around the outside of the cheese box.

10·11 cm

1

2 Use compasses to draw two identical circles on the sheet of card. The circles should be slightly larger than the cheese box.

2

6·7 cm

3 Cut out the circles and glue them to the top and bottom of the cheese box.

3 **4**

4 Use an awl to make a hole through the centre of the **pulley**.

You will find instructions for making these models on the next four pages.

The fixed windmill

You will need: a sheet of thin card about 28 × 28cm, a cork, a straw, a straight piece of coathanger wire about 20cm long, 2 beads, a cardboard box about 22 × 6 × 6 cm, a sheet of card about 20 × 20cm to act as a base, a small **pulley** (see page 12), an egg box and a weathervane (see page 8).

1 Draw a circle with a **radius** of 13cm on the thin card.

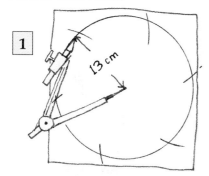

2 Divide the circle into twelve equal sections (see page 7). Cut out the circle.

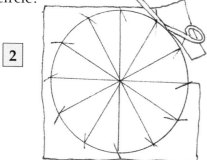

3 Use the same centre point to draw a smaller circle with a **radius** of 5cm.

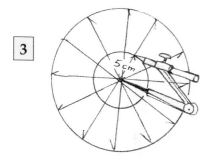

4 Cut along the twelve dividing lines on the large circle as far as the outside edge of the small circle.

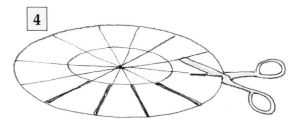

5 Using a knitting needle, score along the **diagonal** of one of the sections and fold up the card along the score line.

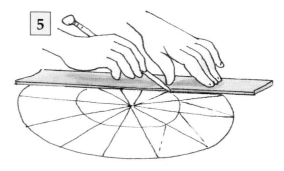

6 Repeat this for the other eleven sections. These are the sails.

7 Glue and tape the cork to the centre of the sails.

8 Glue and tape one end of the cardboard box to the centre of the sheet of card.

9 Make holes in opposite sides of the box at A. Thread the straw through the holes so that a short piece of the straw sticks out at either side as a **bearing**. Glue and tape the straw in position.

12 Slide a bead on to the end of the wire. Push a small **pulley** (see page 12) on to the wire behind the bead. Make a **right-angled** bend in the end of the wire as shown and tape it to the **pulley**.

13 To make a spire for your windmill, cut a section from the egg box. Glue the spire to the top of the windmill.

14 Make a weathervane (see page 8). Push the weathervane into the top of the spire.

10 Push the coathanger wire through the centre of the sails and into the cork. You may need to make a hole in the cork with an awl.

11 Thread a bead on to the coathanger wire to act as a **washer**. Slide the wire through the straw at A.

The wind-powered roundabout

You will need: a piece of card about 9 × 9cm, a toilet roll tube, a strong square box about 16 × 16 × 5cm with lid, a sheet of heavy card to act as a base about 30 × 30cm, a straight piece of coathanger wire about 10cm long, 4 dowel rods each about 22cm long, 90cm of thick wool, a bead, a cork and a large **pulley** (see page 13).

1 Draw and cut out a card circle with a **radius** of 4cm. Make a hole in the centre of the circle with an awl.

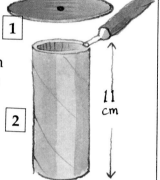

2 Glue the circle on to one end of the toilet roll tube.

3 Tape the other end of the tube to the centre of the upturned square box.

4 Tape the square box to the centre of the sheet of heavy card.

5 Make a hole in each corner of the box as shown. Glue a dowel rod into each hole.

6 Glue the box lid on to the top of the dowel rods.

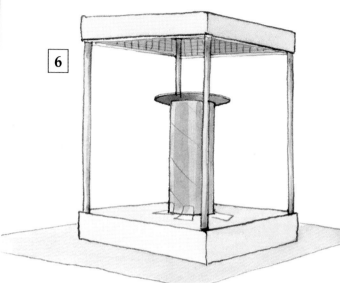

7 Push the cork on to one end of the 10cm length of coathanger wire.

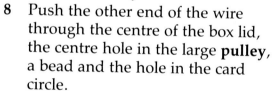

8 Push the other end of the wire through the centre of the box lid, the centre hole in the large **pulley**, a bead and the hole in the card circle.

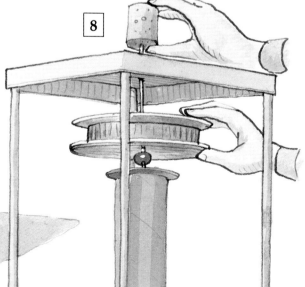

9 Make four horses or other rides for your roundabout. You will find ideas on page 31. Use strips of card to attach the rides to the large **pulley**.

10 Join the **pulley** on the windmill to the **pulley** on the roundabout with a 90cm length of thick wool.

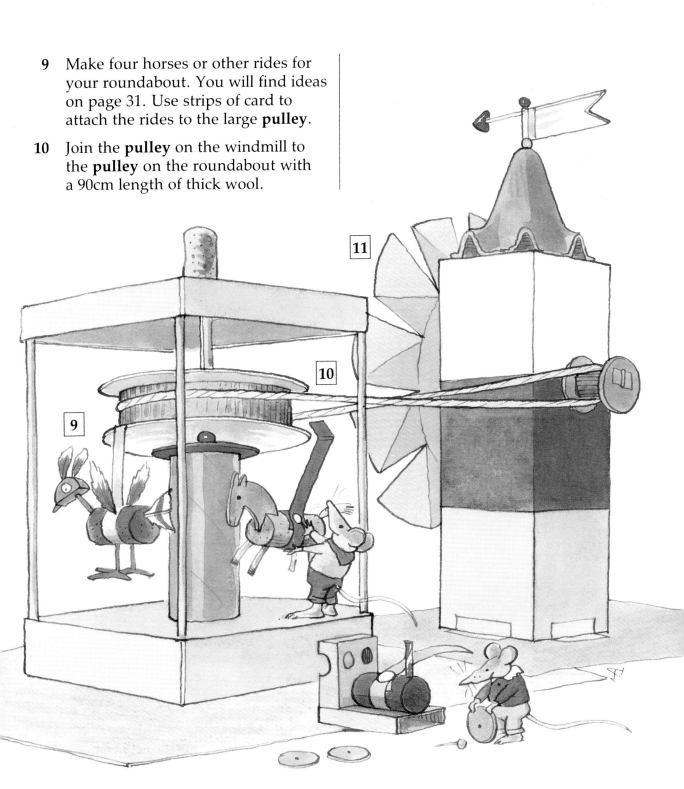

11 Turn the sails of the windmill to drive the roundabout.

12 Try putting your wind-powered roundabout outside. You will need to put stones around the base to stop it blowing away.

Water power

The powerful force of water can be used to turn a waterwheel. As the waterwheel turns, it drives machinery inside the mill. In the past, waterwheels were often used in factories where thread was spun and woven into cloth.

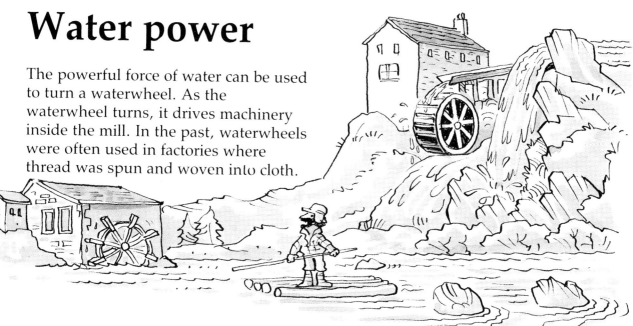

The "overshot" waterwheel

The most efficient type of waterwheel is called an "overshot" wheel. This means that the water is fed in at the top of the wheel. The weight of the water falling on the wheel makes the wheel turn.

> You will need: a plastic lemonade bottle with a lid, a plastic straw, a large round plastic lid with a diameter of 15cm, a large cork, 10 soft plastic film cans, paper fasteners, two 4-litre plastic ice-cream containers, a straight piece of coathanger wire about 20cm long and a large plastic rectangular bowl to catch the water.

1 Cut the lemonade bottle in half.

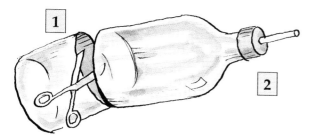

2 Make a hole in the centre of the bottle top with an awl. Glue the straw halfway through the hole.

3 Make a hole through the centre of the plastic lid and the cork with an awl. Attach the cork to the centre of the lid with tacks, making sure you match up the holes.

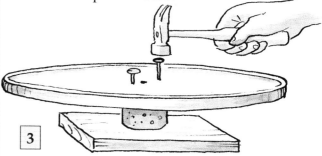

4 Cut a thumb-size piece out of one side of each of the ten film cans.

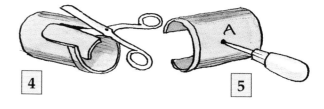

5 Make a small hole with an awl in the other side of each of the film cans at A.

6 Use an awl to make ten holes equally spaced round the rim of the plastic lid as shown. The holes should be far enough apart to allow a film can to sit over each hole, with space between the cans.

7 Match up the holes in the film cans with the holes around the plastic lid. Fasten each can to the lid with a paper fastener. All the cans should point in the same direction.

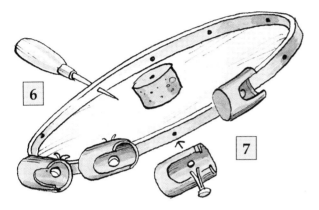

8 Cut holes in the two ice-cream containers as shown. The round hole in the base of box 1 should be large enough for the neck of the lemonade bottle to fit inside.

9 Make a small hole in each side of box 2 at B.

BOX 1

BOX 2

B
B ← 13 cm
13 cm

10 Hold the waterwheel in the centre of box 2 so that the inside film cans have their open ends upwards. Thread the coathanger wire through one of the holes at B, then through the waterwheel and through the hole in the other side of the box. The waterwheel should hang freely in the centre of the box.

11 Use sticky tape to fit the two ice-cream boxes together.

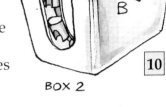

BOX 2

12 Fit the neck of the lemonade bottle into the hole in the top of box 1. Tape the bottle in position so that the straw is above the open cans.

13 Place your waterwheel in the plastic bowl. Pour water into the bottle and watch your wheel begin to turn.

BOX 1

BOX 2

Everything must be waterproof

The weight of the water turns the wheel

Water and pulley power

If you make a **pulley** for your
waterwheel (see page 18) you can use it
to power the Ferris wheel shown here,
the roundabout (see page 16), or any
other model with a **pulley**.

The small **pulley** on the waterwheel is attached to the large **pulley** on the Ferris wheel. As the waterwheel turns, it makes the Ferris wheel turn too.

The water-powered Ferris wheel

You will need: 4 strips of strong card 27 × 3cm, a large matchbox, 30cm of strong wire, a large **pulley** (see p 13), 12 lengths of thin wire 10cm long, 6 toilet roll tubes or other cardboard tubes, a box 16 × 10 × 3cm, a strong piece of card to act as a base about 30 × 30cm, a drinking straw, 4 small matchboxes, 1m of thick wool and some string.

1 Make three holes in each strip of card in the positions shown.

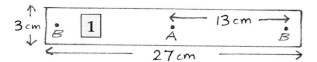

2 Glue two strips together, so that they make a cross. Make sure you match up the holes at A in the centre of each strip.

3 Do the same with the other two strips.

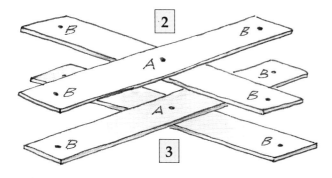

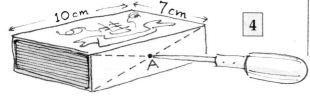

4 Make a hole in the centre of each long side of the large matchbox at A. The holes should be directly opposite each other.

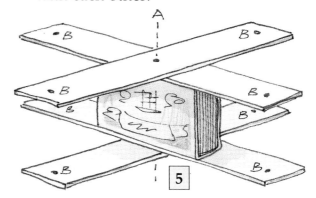

5 Glue the crosses to the sides of the matchbox, lining up the centre holes. The card-crosses should be lined up with each other.

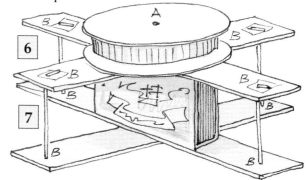

6 Make a large **pulley** (see page 13) and glue it on to the top cross, lining up the centre holes.

7 Join the top and bottom crosses together by threading thin wire through each pair of holes at B. Secure the ends by bending and taping the wire to each cross.

8 Tape the toilet roll tubes together to make two towers. Make two holes at one end of each tower at C. Each tower should be about 33cm high.

9 Glue the box to the centre of your cardboard base. Glue and tape a tower to each side of the box.

10 Make two holes in each tower, at D, 26cm above the base. Thread a half-straw through each pair of holes.

11 Use the trays from the four small matchboxes to make swingboats for your Ferris wheel. Tape a 10cm piece of wire to the long sides of each tray. Bend the top ends of the wires as shown.

12 Hold your Ferris wheel between the towers. Thread the 30cm length of wire through the straws at D, threading the Ferris wheel on as you go. The wire acts as an **axle**. Push a slice of cork on to each end of the **axle** to secure the Ferris wheel.

13 Hook the swingboats on to the bars of the Ferris wheel as shown.

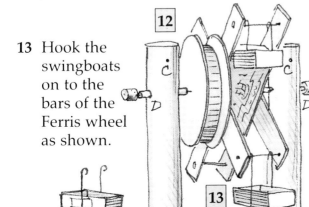

14 Thread a piece of string through each pair of holes in the towers at C. Tape the ends of the string to the base of the model, one at each corner. This will help to strengthen the towers.

15 Add a cone-shaped card roof to the top of each tower. Attach a flag to each roof. Make little people for the swingboats (see page 30).

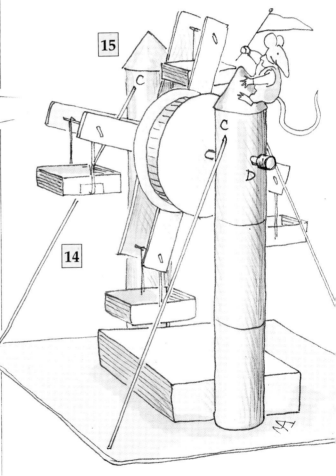

16 Make a small **pulley** (see page 12) and push it on to one end of the wire which runs through the waterwheel. Look at page 20. Join the **pulley** on the Ferris wheel to the **pulley** on the waterwheel with a length of thick wool. Pour water into the bottle at the top of the waterwheel to drive the Ferris wheel.

23

Sand power

A waterwheel uses the weight of water to turn the wheel. Fine sand which flows like a liquid can also be used to turn a wheel. **Gravity**, or the weight of the sand, provides the **energy** to make the wheel go round.

This sawmill turns **rotary movement**, the circular movement of the sand wheel, into **reciprocal movement**, the backwards and forwards movement of the saw.

You could use the movement to work a rocking horse or rock a baby's cradle. A carpenter could plane a plank.

Can you think of other models that make use of reciprocal movement?

Try making a sand wheel. You will find the instructions on page 26. You can use it to power a sawmill like this one (see page 28).

24

The sand wheel

Silver sand is fine enough to flow from a "hopper", or funnel, and fill the cups on a wheel. You can buy silver sand from a garden shop.

> You will need: a cork, 2 large paper plates 23cm in diameter, 2 small paper plates 15cm in diameter, a straight piece of coathanger wire about 35cm long, a shoebox with a lid, 2 square boxes (box 1 is about 18 × 25 × 25cm and box 2 is about 18 × 20 × 20cm), a large piece of card about 30 × 50cm to act as a base, 2 drinking straws, a plastic lemonade bottle with a metal lid and a small bag of silver sand.

1 Slice two 1cm pieces from the cork.

2 Glue one of the pieces of cork to the centre of each of the large paper plates.

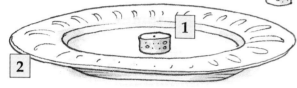

3 Glue and staple a small paper plate to the centre of each large paper plate so that the small plates lie upside-down on top of the large plates as shown.

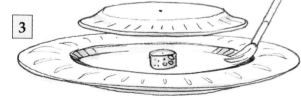

4 Make a hole with an awl through the centre of the cork and plates.

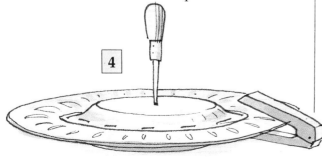

5 Divide the outside edge of one of the large paper plates into twelve equal sections (see page 7).

6 Cut along the section lines as far as the outside edge of the small paper plate.

7 Do the same to the other large plate.

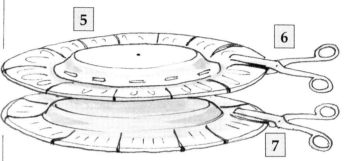

8 Glue the large plates together base to base and thread the coathanger wire through the holes in the centre of the plates.

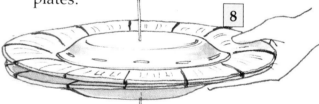

9 Fold in a corner of one of the sections from each plate at A. Staple the corners together to make a "scoop" shape.

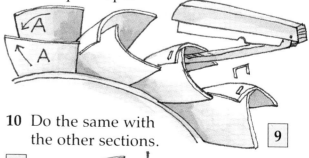

10 Do the same with the other sections.

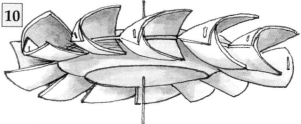

11 Cut a round hole with a diameter of 8cm in the shoebox lid at B. The hole should be large enough for the neck of the lemonade bottle to fit inside.

12 Tape the shoebox lid to box 1. The lid should stick out over one side of the box as shown.

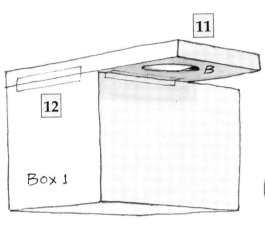

13 Tape the base of box 1 to the top of box 2.

14 Glue and tape the box structure to one end of the cardboard base.

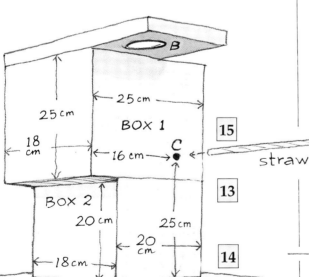

15 Make holes in the opposite sides of box 1 at C. Thread a drinking straw through the holes and tape it in position as a **bearing**.

16 Thread the wire attached to the sand wheel through the holes at C. Push a piece of cork on to the end of the sand wheel wire at D.

17 Cut the bottom off the lemonade bottle. Use an awl to make a small hole in the bottle top.

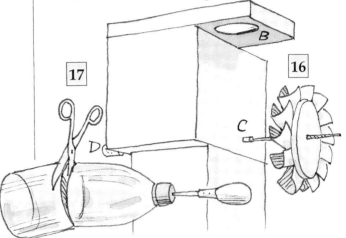

18 Slide the bottle into the hole in the shoebox lid at B. This is the "hopper".

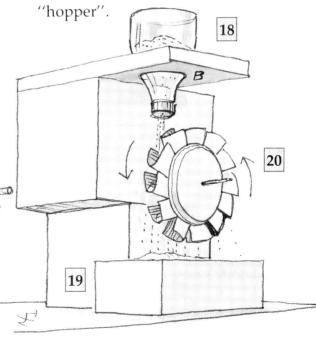

19 Place the shoebox underneath the sand wheel to collect the sand.

20 Fill the "hopper" with sand and watch the sand wheel turn.

The sand-powered sawmill

To make your sand wheel power a sawmill you need to make a card figure with a small card saw.

You will need: a toothpaste box, a large matchbox, card, a table tennis ball, a cork, wool, paper fasteners, a large **pulley** (see page 13), a small **pulley** (see page 12), 35cm of coathanger wire, thick wool about 50cm long and some Plasticine.

1 Draw and cut out arm and leg pieces from the card. The right arm needs to be in two halves joined together at the elbow by a paper fastener.

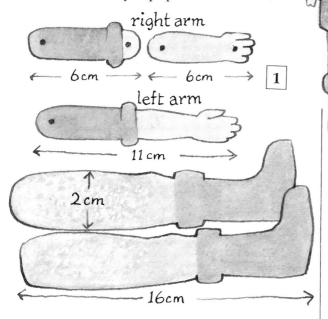

right arm
← 6cm → ← 6cm → 1

left arm
← 11 cm →

2 cm

← 16cm →

2 Make holes in opposite sides of the toothpaste box for the arms and legs at A and B.

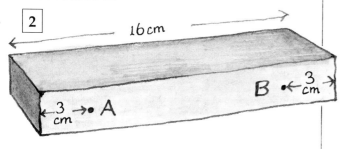

2   ← 16cm →

B •← 3cm →

← 3cm →• A

3 Attach the arms and legs to the box using paper fasteners. The legs are fixed inside the box.

4 Cut out a card saw and attach it to the figure's right hand, using a paper fastener. The saw should be about 25cm long.

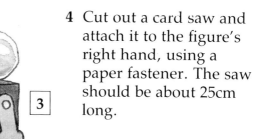

3

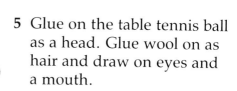

— 25cm —

4

5 Glue on the table tennis ball as a head. Glue wool on as hair and draw on eyes and a mouth.

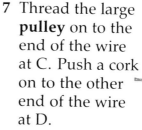

5

6 Make a hole in both sides of the sand mill at C and D and thread the length of coathanger wire through the holes.

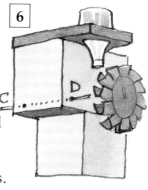

6

C   D

7 Thread the large **pulley** on to the end of the wire at C. Push a cork on to the other end of the wire at D.

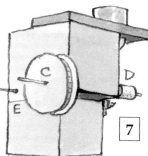

C   D

E

7

28

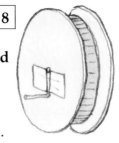

8 Make two **right-angled** bends in the wire sticking out from the large **pulley** and tape the wire to the **pulley**.

9 Glue and tape your figure to the base of the model.

10 Make a small hole in the end of the saw and thread it on to the end of the wire as shown.

11 Make a stand for the saw from the box. Make a Plasticine log and glue it on top of the stand. Position the saw so that the cutting edge lies on top of the Plasticine log as shown.

12 Push the small **pulley** on to the free end of the wire **axle** of the sand wheel at E. Secure the wire by bending and taping it to the **pulley**.

13 Join the two **pulleys** together with a band of thick wool about 50cm long.

14 Pour sand into the "hopper". As the sand runs into the cups on one side of the sand wheel, the wheel will start to turn and the saw will start to cut through the Plasticine log.

People

Use corks, bottle tops, matchsticks and bits of card to make little people and animals. Here are some ideas to help you.

Pipe cleaner figures

1 Make a figure by twisting two pipe cleaners together.

2 Sew on or glue a covered button for the head. Draw on a face with felt pens. Sew or glue on wool for hair.

3 Make clothes from pieces of felt.

Cork figures

1 Use corks of different shapes and sizes to make bodies and heads. Join the corks together with pins or glue.

2 Use pipe cleaners or wire for arms.

3 Use bottle tops for hats. Cut clothes from tissue paper, and glue these on to the cork bodies.

Egg-box figures

1 Cut out a piece of egg-box, and use this for the body. Glue on a bead for the head.

2 Use pipe cleaners or wire for arms.

3 Make clothes from felt and tissue paper.

Roundabout rides

A horse

1 Glue four matchsticks to a cork to make the horse's legs.

2 Draw and cut out a head from card. Make a slit in the cork and slide the head in. Glue in position.

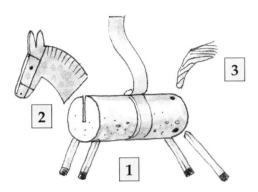

3 Glue on strands of wool for a tail.

4 Attach your horse to the roundabout following the instructions on page 17.

Other animals and birds can be made from corks, feathers, drinking straws and wool.

To decorate your animals, first paint the corks white then paint on suitable markings.

An engine

1 Take the tray out of a small matchbox.

2 Cut the top of the matchbox sleeve a little way up two of the long sides. Fold up the cut piece.

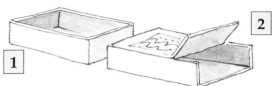

3 Cut two holes in the base of the tray at A. Cut a semicircle in each side at B. Glue the tray inside one end of the matchbox.

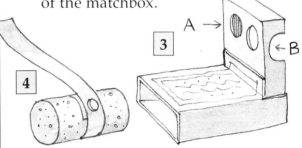

4 Wrap a thin strip of card around the cork. Fix it with a drawing pin.

5 Glue the cork on to the top of the matchbox. Glue a 3cm length of straw on to the front of the cork.

6 Cut four small card circles. Push each circle on to a pin. Push the pins into the base of the matchbox, for wheels.

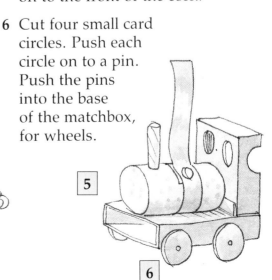

31

Decorating your models

Decorating is easier if you paint all over the models with emulsion paint first.

Put on the details with felt pens or paints.

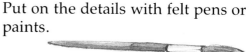

You can decorate the buildings by gluing on cut-out designs from paper or card.

If the surfaces are waxy, or if there are many taped joins, paste paper all over a model before painting it. As well as making any joined pieces stronger, this also makes painting easier.

The models look better if you finish them off with railings of matchsticks and cone-shaped roofs with flags.

pattern for roof cone

glue